HOW TO TEACH WEIGHTLIFTING

IN

HIGH SCHOOL AND COLLEGE

By Carl Miller

SUNSTONE
PRESS
SANTA FE

Sunstone books may be purchased for educational, business, or sales promotional use.
For information please write: Special Markets Department, Sunstone Press,
P.O. Box 2321, Santa Fe, New Mexico 87504-2321.
Printed on acid-free paper
∞

Library of Congress Cataloging-in-Publication Data

(On File)

————————————————

WWW.SUNSTONEPRESS.COM
SUNSTONE PRESS / POST OFFICE BOX 2321 / SANTA FE, NM 87504-2321 /USA
(505) 988-4418 / ORDERS ONLY (800) 243-5644 / FAX (505) 988-1025

TO

FRANK SPELLMAN, OLYMPIC MIDDLEWEIGHT WEIGHTLIFTING

CHAMPION, 1948

who as my former coach, contributed to my basic thinking in weightlifting

and to

HERNAN AGUIRRE, COLOMBIAN NATIONAL AND SOUTH AMERICAN

LIGHTWEIGHT WEIGHTLIFTING CHAMPION

who posed for all the weightlifting pictures

and to

MY TEACHERS AT THE UNIVERSITY OF CALIFORNIA AT BERKELEY AND

THE UNIVERSITY OF ARIZONA

who gave me a thorough knowledge of physiology, kinesiology and anatomy

FOREWORD

This book contains one of the most enlightening physical educating systems that will be your pleasure to read, practice, and enjoy. Carl has gone more thoroughly into the preliminary reasons for using weights and their results than has the author of any other book on weightlifting which I have read. Not only has Carl written this book, but he has also practiced for years all that has been written. Many months and years of experimentation and coordinated college and A. A. U. competition have given Carl an insight as to what can be expected with the application of weights. His insight and recognition of the important way to come around to the end result is most informative.

I first met Carl when he was thirteen years old. He grew into a two hundred pounder of pleasing proportions and a balanced mind, graduating from the University of California and getting his Master's Degree in education at the University of Arizona with a major in physical education.

It is indeed an honour and pleasure to have been a part of Carl's life.

Frank Spellman
Olympic Middleweight Champion 1948

CONTENTS

Introduction – Why Teach the Three Olympic Lifts

The high school or college physical education teacher with the opportunity of teaching the three Olympic lifts may wonder why he should teach these lifts. In a few short paragraphs I would like to present justifications on why these lifts should be taught in a physical education program.

One, the three Olympic lifts comprise an Olympic sport. Competitive weightlifting or just the word weightlifting, which from now on shall mean the three Olympic lifts, is second only to track and field as the most widely participated-in sport in the Olympics as far as number of countries participating is concerned.

Two, interest in weight training in the schools is increasing, and as more and more students train with weights, the interest is growing toward competitive weightlifting. There will not be too many years before there will be interscholastic weightlifting on a large scale. It is present on a small scale now.

Three, in competitive weightlifting, a boy can compete on even bodyweight terms with other boys since there are seven weight classes.

Four, competitive weightlifting develops all the muscles of the body. There is no overdevelopmont of certain parts of the body like that which occurs in some sports where only certain muscles of the body are worked.

Five, competitive weightlifting tests all aspects of being athletic as defined by physical educators. Athletic is usually defined as possessing strength, speed, agility, balance, coordination, flexibility and endurance. The press tests strength, balance, and with the new Russian or Garcy style being used, tests flexibility and coordination. The snatch tests strength, balance, speed, agility, coordination and flexibility. The clean and jerk tests all of the above plus endurance.

Six, the lifts in competitive weightlifting are excellent carry-over activities that a boy can use when he is out of school. They can be done alone as well as with others, thereby not needing partners. The lifts contribute to good body health which includes controlling body weight. And, finally, they can be continued into old age. It is not uncommon to see men in their 60's and 70's weightlifting.

Seven, it is kinesthetically pleasing to weightlift. It is a tingling and wonderful sensation to press, snatch, or clean and jerk a weight. It is like making an over-the-shoulder catch in football, or a 20 foot jump shot in basketball, or a giant in gymnastics.

Eight, competitive weightlifting is relatively free from injuries when compared to other sports. When taught correctly, it gives a boy all the enjoyment of engaging in sports, but he does not receive the injuries that he would, say, in football. It has been pointed out in other books that weightlifting has one of the lowest injury rates of all sports.

Nine, in weightlifting a boy can derive improvement that he can measure. This offers something tangible to a boy at a period of time in his life when he needs something tangible. And if a boy practices, he will get this tangible reward. In almost all cases when a boy begins weightlifting he will get a direct reward for a direct effort.

Ten, teaching competitive weightlifting may open the door to a bright athletic career to some boy. Competitive weightlifting contests are held nationally, and in addition to the Olympics every four years, there are world championships in weightlifting every year.

Eleven, the strength, speed, agility, balance, coordination, flexibility and endurance gained in weightlifting will be of great help in any other sport a boy wishes to undertake.

CHAPTER I

Preliminary Work – 4 to 5 Weeks

Theory of Preliminary Work for Competitive Weightlifting

Competitive weightlifting places a demand on the whole body musculature, so our preliminary work will include working the whole body. We must start out with high repetitions (8 –20) so that the student is not working close to his maximum for one repetition. This will prevent injuries in the early stages of conditioning.

Research tells us that for the most transfer of strength to take place from an exercise to the event that we are training for, we must choose exercises that develop the same movements that are used in the event itself.

Although we start out with high repetitions, we must gradually cut down the number of repetitions and add sets as the preliminary work goes on in order to build strength.

Competitive weightlifting involves being very flexible in the hips, legs and shoulders. It also involves balance, speed, agility, arm to leg coordination, and endurance. So for these reasons part of the preliminary work period will involve the development of these things through light weights or specific calisthenic exercises.

With this theory in mind, I will now present three examples of preliminary work programs. These are designed to fit the most common physical education schedules.

Classes 3 Days a Week, 30-40 Minutes, 5 Weeks

1st Week

1st Workout

All weights are very light.

Conditioning Drills for Weightlifting – 8 to 10 minutes

(1) run 100 to 300 yards   (2) 25 toe touches   (3) deep bouncing squats for 15 seconds (see picture #1)   (4) 2 sets of 10 split squats with each leg forward for one set using no weight (see picture #2)

Introduction of Incline Press or Bench Press – 7 to 10 minutes

Bench Press

Take a shoulder width grip and, with the weight at arms length, lower the weight to the chest taking a deep breath. Pause at the chest for one second and then push as forcefully and as fast as possible, pushing the weight to arms length, letting out the air when the bar is half way up. This push should be like an explosion. Even if the arms finish their extension slowly, the important thing is that you have trained the nerves to react rapidly against resistance. Boys with excess weight do 1 set of 12 to 15 repetitions, and the others do 1 set of 8 to 10 repetitions. (see picture #3).

Incline Press

The same instructions apply here as in the bench press (see picture #4).

Introduction of Upright Row – 7 to 10 minutes

Take a shoulder width grip and, with the arms and back extended, take a deep breath and pull the weight underneath the chin like an explosion. Then lower the weight, letting the air out as it is done. There should be no bending forward of the trunk, and the weight should be lowered to arms extension (see picture #5). Boys with excess weight do 1 set of 12 to 15 repetitions, and the others do 1 set of 8 to 10 repetitions.

Introduction of the Front Squat – 7 to 10 minutes

The bar is resting on the shoulders, and the elbows of the arms are high. The head is slightly up and the feet are shoulder distance apart and slightly turned out. In this position there should be no weight on the arms; all the weight should be on the shoulders (see picture #6). There will be some strain on the wrists but this will usually go away as the tendons of the wrists become looser. If pain in the wrists does not go away or the boy cannot support the bar on his shoulders with the elbows of the arms high, then have him do back squats where the exercise is done with the bar resting on the upper back in the same manner. (The reason for trying to do front squats is that there is less strain on the lower back for beginners.) Now take a deep breath and bend the legs until the tops of the thighs are just below parallel (see picture #7). Explode up until the thighs are extended again. Watch to see that the back stays straight. If it bends, it is usually due to bad form and not to too much weight if light weights are used in the first workout as suggested. Boys with excess weight do 1 set of 15 – 20 repetitions, and the others do 1 set of 10 – 12 repetitions.

2 nd Workout

All weights are still very light.

Conditioning Drills for Weightlifting – 8 to 10 minutes

(1) run 100 to 300 yards for one set using no weights (2) 2 sets of split squats with each leg forward (3) trunk to thigh touches with foot on bench, 10 times each leg (see picture # 8) (4) 10 shoulder dislocates (see pictures # 9 ,10)

Bench Press or Incline Press – 5 to 7 minutes

Boys with excess weight do 2 sets of 12 – 15 repetitions, and the others do 2 sets of 8 – 10 repetitions.

Upright Row – 5 to 7 minutes

Boys with excess weight do 2 sets of 12 – 15 repetitions, and the others do 2 sets of 8 - 10 repetitions.

Front Squats – 5 to 7 minutes

Boys with excess weight do 2 sets of 15 - 20 repetitions, and the others do 2 sets of 10 - 12 repetitions.

In between all sets the rest period should be 1 to 2 minutes. In the future, unless mentioned otherwise, the rest periods will be 1 to 2 minutes. Since the rest of the workout is unoccupied by weight exercises, it is recommended that the teacher lead the class in various stretching exercises.

3 rd Workout

Weights can be increased slightly.

Conditioning Drills for Weightlifting – 8 to 10 minutes

(1) run 200 to 400 yards   (2) 10 shoulder dislocates   (3) 2 sets of 10 split squats with each leg forward for one set using no weight   (4) 10 feet-crossed toe touches (see picture #11)   (5) 25 bicycle pumps (see picture #12)   (6) 10 squat jumps (see pictures #13,14)

Bench Press or Incline Press – 8 to 10 minutes

Boys with excess weight do 3 sets of 12 - 15 repetitions, and the others do 3 sets of 8 - 10 repetitions.

Upright Row – 8 to 10 minutes

Boys with excess weight do 3 sets of 12 - 15 repetitions, and the others do 3 sets of 10 - 12 repetitions.

Front Squats – 8 to 10 minutes

Boys with excess weight do 3 sets of 15 - 20 repetitions, and the others do 3 sets of 10 - 12 repetitions.

2 nd Week

The same workout is used this week as the 3 rd workout of the 1 st week, with the following exceptions. Do the split squats in the conditioning drills with the bar first in the clean position (see picture #15) and then in the snatch position (see picture #16). The last workout of the week do overhead squats with the bar (see picture #17). This will take place of the shoulder dislocates. In the assigned weight exercises choose a weight for the second and third series that is heavy enough so that the boy can just barely do the last repetition. The first series is always comparatively light.

3 rd Week

7 th Workout

Conditioning Drills for Weightlifting - 8 to 10 minutes
(1) 100 yard jog   (2) two 50 yard sprints   (3) 2 sets of 10 split snatch squats with a bar with each leg forward one set   (4) 10 overhead squats with a bar

Bench Press or Incline Press - 8 to 10 minutes
Boys with excess weight do 3 sets of 10-12 repetitions, and the others do 3 sets of 6 - 8 repetitions.

Upright Row - 8 to 10 minutes
Boys with excess weight do 3 sets of 10-12 repetitions, and the others do 3 sets of 8 - 10 repetitions.

Front Squats - 8 to 10 minutes
Boys with excess weight do 3 sets of 10-12 repetitions, and the others do 3 sets of 8 - 10 repetitions.

8 th Workout

Conditioning Drills for Weightlifting - 8 to 10 minutes
(1) 100 yard jog   (2) two 50 yard sprints   (3) 2 sets of 10 split clean squats with a bar with each leg forward for one set   (4) 10 jumping alternate splits (see pictures #18, 19)   (5) throw arms to chest 10 times as split 10 times alternating front leg (see pictures #20, 21)
The rest of the workout is the same as in the 7 th workout.

9 th Workout

Conditioning Drills for Weightlifting - 8 to 10 minutes

(1) 100 yard jog   (2) three 50 yard sprints   (3) 10 overhead squats with bar
(4) 10 squat jumps   (5) throw arms overhead 10 times as squat 10 times (see pictures #22, 23)

The rest of the workout is the same as the 7th workout.

4th Week

10th Workout

Conditioning Drills for Weightlifting – 8 to 10 minutes

(1) 100 yard jog   (2) four 25 yard sprints   (3) bouncing front squats with light weight for 15 seconds (see picture #24)   (4) throw arms to chest 10 times as squat 10 times (see pictures #25, 26)

Bench Press or Incline Press – 10 to 12 minutes

Boys with excess weight do 4 sets of 8 – 10 repetitions, and the others do 4 sets of 4 – 6 repetitions.

Upright Row –10 minutes

Boys with excess weight do 4 sets of 8 – 10 repetitions, and the others do 4 sets of 4 – 6 repetitions.

Front Squats – 10 to 12 minutes

Boys with excess weight do 4 sets of 8 – 10 repetitions, and the others do 4 sets of 4 – 6 repetitions.

11th Workout

Conditioning Drills for Weightlifting – 8 to 10 minutes

(1) 100 yard jog   (2) four 25 yard sprints   (3) 2 sets of 10 split snatch squats with light weight with each leg forward for one set   (4) throw arms overhead 10 times as split 10 times alternating front leg (see pictures #27, 28)

The rest of the workout is the same as the 10th workout.

12th Workout

Conditioning Drills for Weightlifting – 8 to 10 minutes

(1) 100 yard jog   (2) five 25 yard sprints   (3) 2 sets of 10 split clean squats

with light weight with each leg forward for one set   (4) 10 jumping alternate splits
(5) throw arms to chest 10 times as split 10 times alternating front legs
The rest of the workout is the same as the 10th workout.

5 th Week

13th Workout

Conditioning Drills for Weightlifting – 8 to 10 minutes

(1) 100 yard jog   (2) five 10 yard sprints   (3) 10 overhead squats with light
weight   (4) 10 jump squats   (5) throw arms overhead 10 times as squat 10
times

Bench Press or Incline Press – 10 to 12 minutes

Everybody does 4 sets of 4 – 6 repetitions.

Upright Row – 10 minutes

Everybody does 4 sets of 4 – 6 repetitions.

Front Squats – 10 to 12 minutes

Everybody does 4 sets of 4 – 6 repetitions.

14th Workout

Conditioning Drills for Weightlifting – 8 to 10 minutes

(1) 100 yard jog   (2) five 20 yard sprints   (3) bouncing front squats with
light weight for 15 seconds   (4) throw arms to chest 10 times as squat 10 times
The rest of the workout is the same as the 13th workout.

15th Workout

Conditioning Drills for Weightlifting – 8 to 10 minutes

(1) 100 yard jog   (2) five 20 yard sprints   (3) 2 sets of 10 split snatch squats
with light weight with each leg forward for one set   (4) throw arms overhead
10 times as split 10 times alternating front legs
The rest of the workout is the same as the 13th workout.

Classes 2 Days a Week, 45-60 Minutes, 5 Weeks

The exercises used here are the same as in the 3 day a week schedule only arranged in a different order. All references to pictures or exercise explanations should be made by looking back to that schedule. Again, the rest period is 1 to 2 minutes between weight exercises.

1 st Week

1 st Workout

All weights are very light.

Conditioning Drills for Weightlifting – 15 minutes

(1) 100 to 300 yard run   (2) 25 toe touches   (3) deep bouncing squats for 15 seconds   (4) trunk to thigh touches with foot on bench, 10 times each leg
(5) 2 sets of 10 split squats with each leg forward for one set using no weight
(6) 10 shoulder dislocates

Introduction of Bench Press or Incline Press – 10 to 13 minutes

Boys with excess weight do 2 sets of 12-15 repetitions, and the others do 2 sets of 8-10 repetitions.

Introduction of Upright Row – 10 to 13 minutes

Boys with excess weight do 2 sets of 12-15 repetitions, and the others do 2 sets of 8-10 repetitions.

Introduction of Front Squats – 10 to 13 minutes

Boys with excess weight do 2 sets of 15-20 repetitions, and the others do 2 sets of 10-12 repetitions.
It is suggested to let the class go early this day. More exercises would make the students too sore.

2 nd Workout

Weights are still very light.

Conditioning Drills for Weightlifting - 15 minutes

(1) run 200 to 400 yards   (2) trunk to thigh touches with foot on bench, 10 times each leg   (3) 2 sets of 10 split squats with each leg forward for one set using no weight   (4) 10 shoulder dislocates   (5) 25 bicycle pumps   (6) 10 squat jumps   (7) deep bouncing squats for 15 seconds

Bench Press or Incline Press - 12 to 14 minutes

Boys with excess weight do 4 sets of 12-15 repetitions, and the others do 4 sets of 8-10 repetitions.

Upright Row - 12 to 14 minutes

Boys with excess weight do 4 sets of 12-15 repetitions, and the others do 4 sets of 8-10 repetitions.

Front Squats - 12 to 14 minutes

Boys with excess weight do 4 sets of 15-20 repetitions, and the others do 4 sets of 10-12 repetitions.

2 nd Week

The same workout is used this week as the 2 nd workout of the first week with the following exceptions. Do the split squats in the conditioning drills with the bar first in the split clean position and then with the bar in the split snatch position. The last workout of the week do overhead squats with the bar. This will take the place of the shoulder dislocates. In the assigned weight exercises choose a weight for the second, third and fourth sets that is heavy enough so that the boy can just barely do the last repetition. The first series is always comparatively light.

3 rd Week

5 th Workout

Conditioning Drills for Weightlifting - 15 minutes

(1) 100 yard jog   (2) two 50 yard sprints   (3) 10 squat jumps   (4) 2 sets of 10 split snatch squats with a bar with each leg forward for one set   (5) 2

sets of 10 split clean squats with a bar with each leg forward for one set
(6) throw arms to chest 10 times as split 10 times alternating front legs

Bench Press or Incline Press – 12 to 14 minutes

Boys with excess weight do 4 sets of 10 – 12 repetitions, and the others do 4 sets of 6 – 8 repetitions.

Upright Row – 12 to 14 minutes

Boys with excess weight do 4 sets of 10 – 12 repetitions, and the others do 4 sets of 6 – 8 repetitions.

Front Squats – 12 to 14 minutes

Boys with excess weight do 4 sets of 10 – 12 repetitions, and the others do 4 sets of 8 – 10 repetitions.

6 th Workout

Conditioning Drills for Weightlifting – 15 minutes

(1) 100 yard jog   (2) three 50 yard sprints   (3) 10 overhead squats with a bar   (4) 10 jump squats   (5) throw arms overhead 10 times as squat 10 times
(6) 2 sets of 10 split squats with no weight with each leg forward for one set
(7) throw arms overhead 10 times as split 10 times alternating front legs
(8) throw arms to chest 10 times as split 10 times alternating front legs
The rest of the workout is the same as the 5 th workout.

4 th Week

7 th Workout

Conditioning Drills for Weightlifting – 10 to 12 minutes

(1) 100 yard jog   (2) four 25 yard sprints   (3) bouncing front squats with light weight for 15 seconds   (4) throw arms to chest 10 times as squat 10 times
(5) 2 sets of 10 repetitions in the split snatch squat with light weights with each leg forward for 1 set   (6) throw arms overhead 10 times as split 10 times alternating front legs

Bench Press or Incline Press - 14 to 16 minutes

Boys with excess weight do 5 sets of 8 - 10 repetitions, and the others do 5 sets of 4 - 6 repetitions.

Upright Row - 14 to 16 minutes

Boys with excess weight do 5 sets of 8 - 10 repetitions, and the others do 5 sets of 4 - 6 repetitions.

Front Squats - 14 to 16 minutes

Boys with excess weight do 5 sets of 8 - 10 repetitions, and the others do 5 sets of 4 - 6 repetitions.

8 th Workout

Conditioning Drills for Weightlifting - 10 to 12 minutes

(1) 100 yard jog   (2) five 25 yard sprints   (3) 2 sets of 10 split clean squats with light weight with each leg forward 1 set   (4) 10 jumping alternating splits (5) throw arms to chest 10 times as split 10 times alternating front legs
The rest of the workout is the same as the 7 th workout.

5 th Week

9 th Workout

Conditioning Drills for Weightlifting - 10 to 12 minutes

(1) 100 yard jog   (2) five 20 yard sprints   (3) bouncing front squats for 15 seconds with light weights   (4) 10 jump squats   (5) 10 overhead squats with light weight   (6) throw arms overhead 10 times as squat 10 times

Bench Press or Incline Press - 14 to 16 minutes

Upright Row - 14 to 16 minutes

Front Squats - 14 to 16 minutes

Everybody does 5 sets of 4 - 6 repetitons for each exercise.

10th Workout

Conditioning Drills for Weightlifting - 10 to 12 minutes

(1) 100 yard jog   (2) five 20 yard sprints   (3) bouncing front squats with light weight, 2 sets for 15 seconds each

The rest of the workout is the same as the 9 th workout.

Classes 4 Days a Week, 30 — 40 Minutes, 4 Weeks

Most of the exercises used here are the same as in the 3 day a week schedule only arranged in a different order. All references to pictures or exercise explanations used before should be made by looking back to that schedule. As before, unless stated otherwise, the rest period is 1 to 2 minutes between sets.

1 st Week

1 st Workout

All weights are very light.

Conditioning Drills for Weightlifting - 8 to 10 minutes

(1) run 100 to 300 yards   (2) 25 toe touches   (3) deep bouncing squats for 15 seconds   (4) 2 sets of 10 split squats with each leg forward for 1 set using no weight

Introduction of Bench Press or Incline Press - 7 to 10 minutes

Boys with excess weight do 1 set of 12 - 15 repetitions, and the others do 1 set of 8 - 10 repetitions.

Introduction of Upright Row - 7 to 10 minutes

Boys with excess weight do 1 set of 12 - 15 repetitions, and the others do 1 set of 8 - 10 repetitions.

Introduction of Front Squats - 7 to 10 minutes

Boys with excess weight do 1 set of 15 - 20 repetitions, and the others do 1 set of 10 - 12 repetitions.

2 nd Workout

All weights are still very light.

Conditioning Drills for Weightlifting – 8 to 10 minutes

(1) run 100 to 300 yards   (2) 2 sets of 10 split squats with each leg forward for 1 set using no weight   (3) trunk to thigh touches with foot on bench, 10 times each leg   (4) 10 shoulder dislocates

Bench Press or Incline Press – 5 to 7 minutes

Boys with excess weight do 2 sets of 12 – 15 repetitions, and the others do 2 sets of 8 – 10 repetitions.

Introduction of Two Arms Curl – 7 to 10 minutes

Take a shoulder width grip and, with the back and arms extended, take a deep breath and flex the lower arm until the bar is underneath the chin. Letting the air out, lower the weight. There should be no bending forward of the trunk, and the weight should be lowered to arms extension. Boys with excess weight do 1 set of 12 – 15 repetitions, and the others do 1 set of 8 – 10 repetitions (see picture #29). The rest of the workout should be used to do stretching exercises.

3 rd Workout

All weights are still very light.

Conditioning Drills for Weightlifting – 8 to 10 minutes

(1) run 100 to 300 yards   (2) 10 shoulder dislocates   (3) 2 sets of of 10 split squats with each leg forward for 1 set using no weight   (4) 10 feet-crossed toe touches   (5) 10 squat jumps

Upright Row – 5 to 7 minutes

Boys with excess weight do 2 sets of 12 – 15 repetitions, and the others do 2 sets of 8 – 10 repetitions.

Front Squats – 7 – 10 minutes

Boys with excess weight do 2 sets of 15 – 20 repetitions, and the others do 2 sets of 10 – 12 repetitions.

The rest of the workout should be used to do stretching exercises.

4 th Workout

Weights can be increased slightly.

Conditioning Drills for Weightlifting – 8 to 10 minutes

(1) 10 shoulder dislocates (2) 2 sets of split snatch squats with a bar with
each leg forward for 1 set (3) 2 sets of split clean squats with a bar with
each leg forward for 1 set (4) 25 bicycle pumps

Bench Press or Incline Press – 8 to 10 minutes

Boys with excess weight do 3 sets of 12 – 15 repetitions, and the others do 3
sets of 8 – 10 repetitions.

Two Arm Curl – 5 to 7 minutes

Boys with excess weight do 2 sets of 12 – 15 repetitions, and the others do 2
sets of 8 – 10 repetitions.

The rest of the workout should be used to do stretching exercises.

2 nd Week

5 th Workout

Conditioning Drills for Weightlifting – 8 to 10 minutes

This is the same as in the 4 th workout.

Upright Row – 8 to 10 minutes

Boys with excess weight do 3 sets of 12 – 15 repetitions, and the others do 3
sets of 8 – 10 repetitions.

Front Squats – 8 to 10 minutes

Boys with excess weight do 3 sets of 15 – 20 repetitions, and the others do 3
sets rest of 10 – 12 repetitions.

The rest of the workout should be used to do stretching exercises.

6 th Workout

For the rest of the workouts in the assigned weight exercises choose a weight for every set except the first set (this should always be comparatively light) that is heavy enough so that the boy can just barely do the last repetition.

Conditioning Drills for Weightlifting – 8 to 10 minutes

This is the same as in the 4 th workout except do overhead squats with a bar in place of shoulder dislocates.

Bench Press or Incline Press – 8 to 10 minutes

Boys with excess weight do 3 sets of 12 – 15 repetitions, and the others do 3 sets of 8 – 10 repetitions.

Two Arms Curl – 8 to 10 minutes

Boys with excess weight do 3 sets of 12 – 15 repetitions, and the others do 3 sets of 8 – 10 repetitions.

The rest of the workout should be used to do stretching exercises.

7 th Workout

Conditioning Drills for Weightlifting – 8 to 10 minutes

(1) 100 yard jog   (2) two 50 yard sprints   (3) 2 sets of 10 split snatch squats with a bar with each leg forward for 1 set

Upright Row – 10 to 12 minutes

Boys with excess weight do 4 sets of 10 – 12 repetitions, and the others do 4 sets of 6 – 8 repetitions.

Front Squats – 10 to 12 minutes

Boys with excess weight do 4 sets of 10 – 12 repetitions, and the others do 4 sets of 8 – 10 repetitions

8 th Workout

Conditioning Drills for Weightlifting – 8 to 10 minutes

(1) 100 yard jog   (2) two 50 yard sprints   (3) 2 sets of 10 split clean squats

with a bar with each leg forward 1 set   (4) 10 jumping alternate splits

(5) throw arms to chest 10 times as split 10 times alternating front legs

Bench Press or Incline Press – 10 to 12 minutes

Boys with excess weight do 4 sets of 10 - 12 repetitions, and the others do 4 sets of 6 - 8 repetitions.

Two Arms Curl – 10 to 12 minutes

Boys with excess weight do 4 sets of 10 - 12 repetitions, and the others do 4 sets of 6 - 8 repetitions.

3 rd Week

9 th Workout

Conditioning Drills for Weightlifting – 8 to 10 minutes

(1) 100 yard jog   (2) three 50 yard sprints   (3) 10 overhead squats with a bar

(4) 10 squat jumps   (5) throw arms overhead 10 times as squat 10 times

Upright Row – 10 to 12 minutes

Boys with excess weight do 4 sets of 10 - 12 repetitions, and the others do 4 sets of 6 - 8 repetitions.

Front Squats – 10 to 12 minutes

Boys with excess weight do 4 sets of 10 - 12 repetitions, and the others do 4 sets of 8 - 10 repetitions.

10th Workout

Conditioning Drills for Weightlifting – 8 to 10 minutes

(1) 100 yard jog   (2) four 25 yard sprints   (3) bouncing squats for 15 seconds

(4) throw arms to chest 10 times as squat 10 times

Bench Press or Incline Press – 10 to 12 minutes

Boys with excess weight do 4 sets of 10 - 12 repetitions, and the others do 4 sets of 6 - 8 repetions.

Two Arms Curl - 10 to 12 minutes

Boys with excess weight do 4 sets of 10 - 12 repetitions, and the others do 4 sets of 6 - 8 repetitions.

11th Workout

Conditioning Drills for Weightlifting - 8 to 10 minutes

(1) 100 yard jog   (2) four 25 yard sprints   (3) 10 split snatch squats with light weight with each leg forward 1 set   (4) throw arms overhead 10 times as split 10 times alternating front legs

Upright Row - 10 to 12 minutes

Boys with excess weight do 4 sets of 8 - 10 repetitions, and the others do 4 sets of 4 - 6 repetitions.

Front Squats - 10 to 12 minutes

Boys with excess weight do 4 sets of 8 - 10 repetitions, and the others do 4 sets of 6 - 8 repetitions.

12th Workout

Conditioning Drills for Weightlifting - 8 to 10 minutes

(1) 100 yard jog   (2) five 25 yard sprints   (3) 10 jumping alternate splits
(4) throw arms to chest 10 times as split 10 times alternating front legs

Bench Press or Incline Press - 10 to 12 minutes

Boys with excess weight do 4 sets of 8 - 10 repetitions, and the others do 4 sets of 4 - 6 repetitions.

Two Arms Curl - 10 to 12 minutes

Boys with excess weight do 4 sets of 8 - 10 repetitions, and the others do 4 sets of 4 - 6 repetitions.

4 th Week

13th Workout

Conditioning Drills for Weightlifting - 8 to 10 minutes

(1) 100 yard jog   (2) five 20 yard sprints   (3) 10 overhead squats with light weight   (4) throw arms overhead 10 times as squat 10 times

Upright Row - 10 to 12 minutes

Boys with excess weight do 4 sets of 8 - 10 repetitions, and the others do 4 sets of 4 - 6 repetitions.

Front Squats - 10 to 12 minutes

Boys with excess weight do 4 sets of 8 - 10 repetitions, and the others do 4 sets of 6 - 8 repetitions.

14th Workout

Conditioning Drills for Weightlifting - 8 to 10 minutes

(1) 100 yard jog   (2) five 20 yard sprints   (3) bouncing squats with light weights for 15 seconds   (4) throw arms to chest 10 times as squat 10 times

Bench Press or Incline Press - 10 to 12 minutes

Boys with excess weight do 4 sets of 8 - 10 repetitions, and the others do 4 sets of 4 - 6 repetitions.

Two Arms Curl - 10 to 12 minutes

Boys with excess weight do 4 sets of 8 - 10 repetitions, and the others do 4 sets of 4 - 6 repetitions.

15th Workout

Conditioning Drills for Weightlifting - 8 to 10 minutes

(1) 100 yard jog   (2) five 20 yard sprints   (3) 2 sets of 10 split snatch squats with light weight with each leg forward for 1 set

Upright Row – 10 to 12 minutes

Everybody does 4 sets of 4 – 6 repetitions.

Front Squats – 10 to 12 minutes
Everybody does 4 – 6 repetitions.

16th Workout

Conditioning Drills for Weightlifting – 8 to 10 minutes

(1) 100 yard jog   (2) five 20 yard sprints   (3) 10 split clean squats with light weight with each leg forward for 1 set   (4) 10 jumping alternate splits (5) throw arms to chest 10 times as split 10 times alternating front legs

Bench Press or Incline Press – 10 to 12 minutes

Everybody does 4 sets of 4 – 6 repetitions.

Two Arms Curl – 10 to 12 minutes

Everybody does 4 sets of 4 – 6 repetitions.

CHAPTER Ⅱ

The Two Hands Clean and Press

The rules state that there can be a moderate lean back from the vertical once the bar has begun to be pressed. What is moderate lean back? Judges have always had difficulty in reaching agreement on this point. Usually it is safe to say that judges today will pass a style in which the lifter does not lean back farther than 30° from the vertical (see picture # 30). Whatever is moderate lean back, around it lifters have adaped their styles. Generally speaking, this has involved using one of 3 types of styles. In one. the lifter starts in a vertical position and as the bar is going up, leans back. I call this the "start straight and lean back style". This is the style that will be taught since our limited class hours will permit only the teaching of one style. But before continuing, I would like to offer a brief explanation of the other two styles.

Since the rules say that a moderate lean back is permitted, a style which is called the "lean back style" came into being in the late 1940's by Gregory Novak of Russia. In this style the lifter takes a fairly wide grip, assumes a lean back of about 30° immediately after the clean, presses from this position, and receives the referee's signal to put the bar down after completion of the press from this position (see picture #31).

The other style, Garcy style as developed by Tony Garcy of the United States or the Russian Style (both are nearly the same and came into being about the same time), took officials by surprise, and they are still figuring out what to do about it. Slow motion pictures of it show that there is considerable body movement and more than 30° lean back from the vertical. But done in competition, it is so fast that the referee does not know whether or not he saw excess movement and backbend. Upon cleaning the weight, the lifter takes a lay back position with a narrow grip (see picture #32). The chest is back and the hips, thighs and stomach are bowed forward. The knees are locked and the hips and the thighs are tensed very hard. Upon receiving the referee's signal to press, the lifter throws the weight off his chest straight up with the chest coming forward and the hips, thighs and stomach going back (see picture #33). The bar has to be thrown about 2 - 3 inches above the hairline to be able to finish this press fast so that the judges do not catch what is going on. As the weight nears this mark the body goes back to its original position with chest back and hips, thighs and stomach bowed forward (see picture #34). The bar is caught 2 - 3 inches above the hairline. With the resulting momentum and the strength of the triceps, deltoids, and pectoralis muscles, the bar is "pressed" to arms extension and the body comes erect. As was said, this is done with such speed that it is hard to detect. The results of increased press poundages are amazing. A Russian lightweight using this style who held the world record for the press at 297, after making the record was asked what he thought he could press as judged years ago. His reply was "about 226". To say more on the subject goes beyond the scope of this book.

Teaching the Clean for the Press

The Address Press

We will begin the teaching of the clean by starting with the address position. The feet are in line with one another about 4 - 6 inches apart with toes slightly pointed outward. The instep of the feet is directly underneath the bar. The hands and arms are at the sides (see picture #35).

The Get-Ready Position

From the address position the lifter assumes the get-ready position which is with the knees bent, back straight, arms straight, eyes looking forward, shoulder width grip with a hook grip (students will use a hook grip in all the lifts from here on out (see picture #36). In this position the center of gravity is over the bar. Right before the lifter attempts to clean the bar he takes a breath from this position and holds the breath throughout the clean (see picture #37).

First Pull

From the get-ready position the student goes through what is called first pull which is to pull the bar around the top of the knees. This is done by an extension of the legs. It is important to keep the back at nearly the same position as it was in the get-ready position. This first pull is not exceptionally fast. Its use is to bring the bar into good position for the all important second pull (see picture #38).

Second Pull

At the end of the first pull the student is in the best anatomical position to exert pulling force on the bar. When the bar arrives at this position, very forcefully the student rapidly and fully extends his back in simultaneous timing with the extension of the knees and hips, elevation of the shoulders, flexion of the elbows, extension of the head, and plantar flexion of the feet in roughly that order. Naturally there is an overlap of movements. At the end of this pull, the bar should be between nipple and neck height. This marks the end of the second pull in the clean for the press (see picture #39).

Elbow Whip and Dip

At this point there is a forceful throwing of the elbows from a position outside to a position underneath the bar, and at the same time there is a bending (dipping) of the legs (see picture #40). The bar is thus caught at the shoulder (see picture #41). The lifter extends his legs and is in good position to press the bar. The bar is high on the shoulders and is being supported by them. The elbows are forward and slightly out. The eyes are looking forward. The knees are locked. The feet are shoulder distance or a little wider apart (this was done by shuffling the feet out as the legs dipped).

Sequence of Exercises to Teach the Clean for the Press

First Pull Exercise

Go through the first pull with no weight, then with an empty bar, and then with light weights. Do this in series of 4 - 7 repetitions. With no weight and an empty bar rest 30 seconds between sets. With light weights rest 1 - 2 minutes between sets. Check that the back is straight, the bar is close to the body, and the arms are straight.

Second Pull Exercise

Beginning with the starting position of the second pull, go through the second pull in the same exercise sequence as was done for the first pull and with the same rest intervals. Check again that the back is straight and the bar is close to the body. Check also that the arms do not do the pulling and that the back does (see picture #42) If the arms are doing the pulling, it is because they are bending too soon (see picture #43). See also that the back and head are fully extended.

High Pull Exercise – combining first and second pull

Start with a light weight, which would be 10 to 25 pounds above the weight the student was using for his upright rows. Do this exercise 4 sets of 6 repetitions resting 1 - 2 minutes between sets. Pull the bar to chest height or to chin height. Pull all repetitions from the floor. Check that when the bar passes the knees it definitely speeds up. Also check the things that were checked with the first and second pulls (see picture #44).

Elbow Whip and Dip Exercise

Starting in the position where the elbow whip would start (bar between nipple and neck height), go through the elbow whip and dip in the same sequence of exercises as was done with the first pull and with the same rest intervals (see picture #45).

Clean Complete

Combine first and second pull, elbow whip and dip in the same sequence of exercises as was done with the first pull and with the same rest intervals.

Teaching the Press

Grip

To teach the "start straight and lean back style" of press, we must first select a grip on the bar. We say that a grip that is even with the width of the shoulders is the best grip to start with. A narrower grip gives a fast start but is hard to finish. A wider grip is hard to start but easy to finish.

Initial Drive

Assuming the bar is at the shoulders, tense the hips very hard. The breath taken for the clean is still in the body. Push hard with the arms and at the same time the hips and legs move forward as the chest and head move back (see picture #46). The bar should be kept fairly close to the face (see picture #47). This initial drive should bring the bar to the hairline or higher.

Follow Through

With the bar at the hairline level, the body is bent back about 25 to 30 degrees from the vertical. From this point the body does not bend back further or bends back very little. If the hips were tense in the initial drive they are even more tense now as are the thighs. The chin is down and the eyes are looking forward or down. Looking up brings the shoulders too far back with a resulting lack of full support under the bar. The arms then merely straighten to finish the press.

Sequence of Exercises to Teach the Press

Initial Drive Exercise

With no weight go slowly through the coordination of hips and thighs moving forward, head and chest moving back, and arms extending to hairline level. Check that the arms extend to hairline level as the hips and thighs move forward and the head and chest move back. Usually the beginner will move the thighs and hips forward and head and chest back without extending the arms, or he will extend the arms first and then do the rest. The movement of the body and the arms is done simultaneously. Also check that the bar goes straight up and not forward.

Repeat the above movement with speed. When the student does the movement well, he then does the same thing with first an empty bar and then light weights doing 4 - 7 repetitions, resting 30 seconds between sets with the empty bar and 1 - 2 minutes between sets with light weights.

Follow Through Exercise

With no weight, assume position at the end of the initial drive (at hairline or a little higher). Extend arms to full extension. Stress tensing the hips and thighs and keeping the head forward or down and stationary. Air is let out near the top of the extension. Watch that the student does not fall away from the bar (see picture #48) but stays rigid and extends the arms.

As with the initial drive exercise, repeat the above movements with speed. When the student does the movements well, he does the same things with an empty bar and then with light weights doing 4 - 7 repetitions with the same rest intervals as described above.

Complete Press Exercise

Go through the complete press in the same sequence as before, no weight, empty, and then light weights. When light weights are used and if equipment allows it, do this phase by taking the light weights off a stand. This eliminates having to think about cleaning when learning to press. Again do repetitions of 4 - 7 with the same rest intervals.

Combined Clean and Press Exercise

After the student is competent in the press, practice the clean and press in singles. That is to say, clean the bar, press it, and return it to the platform. After the student's form is good, do 1 clean and several presses. Pause and come to starting press position between each press. After letting the air out and the bar is at the top, let the bar down to the chest for another repetition and take another breath as the bar is being lowered. When the student can clean and press the bar several repetitions in good style, he is ready to start a pressing routine designed to improve his press.

Pressing Routines

There are many pressing routines, and we must choose them in accordance with certain factors. One factor is that our objective is to press the most weight for only 1 repetition. Another factor is that we must continue to develop the newly acquired skill. Still another factor is the limited time of the class and the fact that we must also learn the snatch and clean and jerk, plus the fact that we should rest 2 minutes between all sets in which weights are used, whether in pressing, snatching, or clean and jerking. With these factors in mind, the following is a presentation of a beginning routine, and following this will be three example routines that can be followed after the beginning routine is completed.

Beginning Routine - 1 to 2 weeks

Here will be done 4 sets of 6 repetitions. We want the student to progressively use heavier weights with each set. The first set should be very easy, stressing correct form and breathing. The second set, add 10 pounds. The third set, add enough weight so the student does the last repetition with quite a bit of effort. We say that if he had to he could have done one more repetition. The fourth set the student should try to use the same weight as he did in set three. If it is too much, drop back in weight.

As the beginner advances, let him try doing his maximum for 6 repetitions. Do not let him try his maximum every training day, as this will cause a regression. Trying a maximum for 6 repetitions on one training day out of three is a good general rule. Make sure you stress good form to the student always, and he should not advance in weight if his form is bad. At the end of three to four weeks (9-12 training sessions) the teacher may test the student's maximum for 6 repetitions if he cares to since the student will be ready physically for such a test.

After the Beginning Routine

After the beginning routine the student must work closer to his maximum for one repetition. This means cutting down the number of repetitions and increasing the weight and number of sets. As before, the student will use progressively heavier weights with each set. In this type of program, it is important to be sure the student is well warmed up. Two quick sets of 10-15 repetitions of press with very light weights (10-20 pounds) should be adequate. In this type of routine try a maximum for 1 repetition every 1½ to 2 weeks. In accordance with the above statements, here are three example routines.

5 — 4 — 3 — 2 — 1 Routine

The first set is 5 repetitions. They are not unusually hard. Naturally, they are harder than a warm-up, but not exhausting. The second set is done with 4 repetitions. Weight is added and this should be enough weight to have made the 4 repetitions about all the student could do for 4 repetitions. 5 - 10 pounds are added when the student does 3 repetitions, which should be a maximum for 3. The fourth set with 2 repetitions will be a maximum for 2. Again, about 5 - 10 pounds are added. Another 5 - 10 pounds are added for the fifth set and this may or may not be the maximum for 1 repetition.

When a student feels extra good or extra bad he may add more or less weight with each set. Students like to add variety by concentrating during one training session on maximum for a certain amount of repetitions. For example, a student may go relatively light one day on all sets but the fourth, in which he will try a new maximum for 2 repetitions, or he may try the new maximum for 4 repetitions on his second set.

5 — 3 — 1 — 3 — 3 Routine

The first set is not a maximum for 5. The second set is 3 repetitions, using weight that is a little below maximum for 3. The third set of 1 repetition may be a maximum when the student feels good or below maximum when the student feels average or below average. After the third set the student drops back to a lighter weight and tries to do two sets of 3 repetitions. When this can be done, add weight the next time. This next time the student may be able to get one set of three and one set of two; this is okay. After this he tries to get that third repetition.

4 — 3 — 2 — 2 — 4 Routine

The first set is not a maximum for 4. The next set of 3 repetitions is likewise not a maximum for 3. The third set should be the maximum or near maximum for 2, and the fourth set should be done with the same weight as the third if possible. If this can not be done, drop back in weight only as far as need be. When the student feels very good he may go lighter on the third set and try a maximum for 1 on the fourth set. The fifth set is a maximum for 4.

With each of these routines one must work hard but yet not so hard one finds himself regressing. A good practice is to have the student train according to how he feels each training session. Varying in a planned manner the poundage used also gives good results. In this system, a day is picked for doing a maximum, and the student looks forward to this day. For example, one heavy day, one medium day. and then a light day is good. A heavy day means just that. A medium day is 10-15 pounds less on each set. A light day is 20-30 pounds less on each set.

One must remember that maximum weights must be used at times to improve, but remember that the sets in which one is not using maximum weights are also contributing to gains. Style is being improved, which will help the student lift heavier weights and help prevent retroactive inhibition. And at the same time, it is important to remember that using maximum weights all the time has been proven physiologically harmful for gaining strength.

CHAPTER Ⅲ

The Two Hands Snatch

The rules state that the bar shall be pulled in one movement from the ground to the full extension of the arms overhead in a continuous motion while either splitting or squatting under the bar. With this is mind, we will start with the split style and then go on to the squat style.

Teaching the Split Style

There are many forms of the split style of which the equal split, the wedge split, and the hop back split are the most commonly used. Among these, the most popular and also seemingly most efficient is the equal split, which will be our style for teaching. It will be said in passing that the wedge split, in which just the front leg moves and goes forward, has proved very benefical to heavy slow men, and the hop back split, in which just the back leg moves and goes back, has proved very beneficial to lifters who pull the bar back from the vertical (which mathematically is very efficient).

The Address Position

This is the same as in the clean for the press.

The Get-Ready Position

This is the same as in the clean for the press, but the bar is grasped with a grip that is much wider than shoulder distance. The actual distance depends on the tightness of the shoulders. The tighter the shoulders, the wider the grip should be (see picture #49). From the get-ready position the snatch will be taught in terms of first pull, second pull, and so on as was done with the clean for the press.

First Pull

Everything is the same here as in the clean for the press with the exception of the grip on the bar (see picture #50).

Second Pull

What was said about the second pull for the clean for the press can be said here, but remember that the grip is different (see picture #51).

Split and Flip

The flip or turning over of the wrists and the splitting of the legs is done simultaneously (see picture #52). The flip involves only extending the wrists and arms, and the splitting involves moving one leg forward and the other back about equally. The length of split depends on the body structure of the student. He should be as low as possible without touching his back knee to the floor. He should at least reach the position in which the top of the front leg is parallel to the floor. If he does not, he needs more flexibility work for the hips and legs. The student should reach the bottom of his split the same time the flip is completed. If the arms are a little bent after securing the bar after the flip, extend them immediately. In this position the trunk is straight and the hips are directly under the trunk. The head is directly over the trunk with the eyes looking forward. The bar is directly over the head or a little back (see picture #53).

Recovery

Recovery means coming from the split or squat position to the standing position with the bar over the head and the feet in line. The recovery is made when the student has the bar under control and not before. Students often make the mistake of recovering before they have the bar secured. If the bar is too forward, rock forward (move the weight of the body over the front leg). If the bar is too far back, rock back (move the body weight over the rear leg). There are two types of recovery, the back to front and the front to back. The front to back is the better of the two and will be taught here. From the split position the front foot is brought back a little and then the back foot forward a little. The front foot is then brought a little farther back and the back foot a little farther forward. The feet usually are in line now. If not, bring the front foot back a little more (see pictures #54, 55).

Sequence of Exercises to Teach the Split Snatch

Go through the same sequence of exercises in which the student starts with no weight, then uses an empty bar, then light weights, as was done in learning the first pull for the clean for the press, using the same rest intervals.

Flip and Small Split Exercise

Using the same sequence as above, do the following. Assume the position at the end of the second pull, which is with the bar between nipple and neck, and the student is on his toes. Now, extend the wrists and arms, split, and secure the bar. The split is small as the body drops about six inches. Make sure the student does the movement with speed and that he gets the bar over the head and not out in front. It is important that the split is completed at the same time the flip is completed, not one right after the other. The position is the same as in a complete split only higher. Be especially sure the trunk is straight. Do 4 – 7 repetitions with 30 seconds rest between sets when using no weight or an empty bar, and do the same amount of repetitions but with 1 – 2 minutes rest when practicing with light weights.

Power Split Snatch Exercise

The word power used in connection with the pulling for the snatch or clean means securing the bar after the wrist flip before the thighs reach parallel and not sinking lower than parallel after the bar is secured. The student lifts the bar from the platform going through the different phases as he would for a complete snatch. The only difference is that the student makes a small split instead of a deep one. Have the student start with the weight he was using for upright rows, doing 6 repetitions and resting 2 minutes between sets. All the repetitions are done from the platform. Be sure the student is doing things correctly as he passes through the various parts of the lift.

Split Snatch Exercise

Again following the sequence of no weight, bar, light weight, do the split snatch in entirety. When using light weights do sets of 3 repetitions, dead hanging the second and third repetitions with 2 minutes rest between sets. When using no weight and empty bar, do sets of 4 - 7 repetitions. A dead hang consists of the bar being returned to the knees for the repetitions and not the platform (see picture #56). When the student can do this well, he is ready for a split snatch routine.

Split Snatch Routines

As with the press, there are many routines, and the same factors enter into making a routine. A further factor for the snatch is that it is more complicated; thus lighter weight will be used to develop form. The following is a beginning routine. Following this will be three example routines that can be followed after the beginning routine is completed.

Beginning Routine – 1 to 2 weeks

We want the student to do 4 sets of 3 repetitions and then 2 sets of 3 in the high pull with 2 minutes rest between sets. High pull in the snatch is like the high pull in the clean for the press except that the student uses a snatch grip instead of a clean grip. Start the student with the weight he was using for his upright rows and have him do complete snatches in singles and the high pulls in singles (singles means putting the bar down on the platform after each repetition). The student can add weight if he is using good style, but this should not be encouraged. Perfecting style should be emphasized during this training routine. If a student misses twice in a row with a weight or can not get the form with the weight he is using, he must drop down in weight. In the high pulls stress acceleration after the bar gets to the knees.

After the Beginning Routine

Now we must develop pulling power toward lifting a maximum for 1 repetition. Therefore, repetitions must be cut down and weight added, especially with the high pulls which are designed to add power. Do 2 sets of 10 – 15 repetitions with very light weights (10 – 20 pounds) in the snatch to warm up. Continue to stress style, and again if a student misses two times in a row with a weight or can not get the correct form with the weight he is using, he must drop back in weight. However, it should be noted that a maximum will be tried every two weeks since this gives a reference point to the student and he can therefore analyze his mistakes in terms of his ultimate goal of lifting the most weight for 1 repetition. All this time the teacher should stress splitting lower and lower. This means paying attention to flexibility work. Rest periods are 2 minutes between sets.

4 — 3 — 2 — 1 Snatches and 2 Sets of 3 in the High Pull

Start with a light weight and work up in weight in 10 – 15 pound jumps. None of the weights used will be a maximum for the number of repetitions. Dead hang the repetitions. The high pulls should end between nipple and neck height. With a continued learning of the second pull, the student will be using more weight in the high pulls than he can snatch.

2 — 2 — 2 — 2 Snatches and 2 Sets of 3 in the High Pull

The first two sets are considerably below the student's best for 2 repetitions. Using 30 or 40 pounds below his best would not be too low a weight. The third set should be a near maximum for 2 repetitions. The last set may be a maximum for 1 or 2 repetitions when the student feels good. High pulls are done as in the 4 - 3 - 2 - 1 routine.

3 — 3 — 3 — 1 Snatches and 2 Sets of 3 in the High Pull

The first two sets are considerably below the student's best for 3 repetitions. The third set is a near maximum for 3 repetitions. The fourth set can be a maximum for 1 repetition when the student wishes to do his best for 1. Otherwise, it is a weight that can be lifted once consistently and sometimes twice. Again, high pulls are done as in the 4 - 3 - 2 - 1 system.

Teaching the Squat Style

Everything is the same as in the split style through the second pull. As the bar gets to its highest point it must be flipped back as in the split style, but in the squat style the lifter squats under the bar to secure it instead of splitting.

Squat and Flip

Supposedly, the student has risen on his toes after the second pull and has a lot of upward momentum (see picture #57). From here the squatting is a jump-shuffle forward from the toes while the feet move outward at the same time to form a wider base as the knees bend and the lifter goes under the bar. At the same time, the lifter is flipping the bar. Like the flip in the split style, this involves extending the wrists and arms. The extension here is a forcing of the bar back, and the wrists actually extend more than in the split style. Tell the student to push out toward each end of the bar, trying to lengthen it as if it could be stretched. Many squat snatches are lost because the wrists are not extended hard and fast. As the bar is being flipped and secured, the head, which was extended during the second pull, drops and the hips go out in back; thus the trunk inclines forward. How much the hips go out in back and how much the head drops depend on to what position the bar is pulled overhead. Actually, sometimes the hips go forward and the head up; such is the case if the bar is pulled forward. If the bar is pulled back, the head is down and the hips back. This is a balance mechanism (see picture #58).

Recovery

As in the split style, the bar must be secured before coming up. This means not rocking back and forth as in the split snatch, but rather lowering or raising the hips and raising or dropping the head. This is the same process as described above. After the bar is secured, the lifter merely rises from the squat position.

Sequence of Exercises to Teach the Squat Snatch

Shoulder Stretching Exercise

Do at least 2 sets of 10 shoulder dislocates.

Overhead Squat Exercise

The student should do 8 repetitions using 80% of his bodyweight. Practice by doing 4 sets of 8 repetitions starting light and working up in weight with 2 minutes rest between sets. The object here is to obtain the exact balance needed in the squat snatch. Be sure the body is inclined forward with the head down and the hips back. The student should squat all the way to the bottom. This exercise will be difficult especially for the students with tight shoulders. It is hoped that the preliminary work has solved the problem. If tightness persists, take as wide a grip on the bar as possible. With time the shoulders should rotate back, putting the bar in such an anatomical position that it is effortless to hold the bar overhead.

First Pull, Second Pull, High Pull Exercises

As in the split style, go through the sequence of exercises with no weight, empty bar, and finally light weights with the same rest intervals as before.

Flip and Small Squat Exercise

Following the same sequence as above, do the following. Assume the position of the end of the second pull, bar between nipple and neck and the student on his toes. Now he extends the wrists, trying to stretch the bar out while jump-shuffling forward and down under the bar. The student drops only about six inches (see picture #59). This should be done with speed, and the squat is completed the same time as the flip, not one right after the other. Position is the same as in the complete squat only higher. Be especially sure that the weight is back, hips back and head down. Do 4 - 7 repetitions resting 30 seconds when using an empty bar or no weights, and resting 1 - 2 minutes when using light weights.

Power Squat Snatch Exercise

This is the same exercise as the power split snatch except that the student squats instead of splitting. Do sets of 6 repetitions with all the repetitions being done from the platform and starting with the weight that the student used for doing upright rows. Rest 2 minutes between sets.

Squat Snatch Exercise

Use the same sequence as in the split snatch exercise.

Squat Snatch Routine

Beginning Routine - 1 to 2 weeks

Balance and timing seem to be a little more difficult in the squat snatch than in the split snatch for the beginner, so be especially watchful that the student stays with light weights to learn these things. With 2 minutes rest between sets, do 4 sets of 3 repetitions in the squat snatch and 2 sets of 3 in the high pulls. The high pulls can be done with heavy weights if the instructor thinks the student can do them with good form. As the student gets more proficient in the squat style he may adopt any of the 3 routines outlined for the split snatch, following the same principles.

Split or Squat Style?

The purpose of the following discussion is not take a stand on which is the better style but only to present the advantages and disadvantages of each so that the instructor can have a better understanding of the two styles and thus teach them better. What is said here about the split and squat styles for the snatch can be said about the same styles for the clean of the clean and jerk.

Split Style

The advantages of the split style are: (1) A beginner can get a working style with the split faster than he can a working style in the squat snatch. (2) If the bar is pulled too far forward or too far backward, the lifter can use a forward or backward motion to save the lift. This can not be done in the squat style. (3) Students with tight shoulders can use the split style with more efficiency than they can the squat style. (4) Students with very flexible hamstring muscles, hips, and lower back can get extremely low in the split style.

The disadvantages are: (1) A student can not go as low in the split style as in the squat style unless he has extraordinary flexibility in the hamstring muscles, hips and lower back. And if one is that flexible, he has a good chance of going lower in the squat style.

Squat Style

The advantages of the squat style are: (1) The average student can go lower than in the split style. (2) Squatting under the bar is thought to be a less complex movement than splitting under the bar, and if the student has good balance the squat style should be easier to learn. (3) Students with tight hips can go lower in the squat style than in the split style.

The disadvantages are: (1) Because of the additional balance that is needed, it takes longer to learn a working squat style than a working split style. (2) There is little or no forward and back movement under the bar in the squat style, and if the bar is pulled too far forward or backward, there is little chance of saving the lift. (3) Many people do not have the potential in flexibility of the shoulders to do the squat style. When these people do this style they have to hold the bar overhead with sheer muscle which is very inefficient and can not be done with heavy weights.

CHAPTER Ⅳ

Two Hands Clean and Jerk

This is the lift that many people say separates the men from the boys because it combines the power that is highly exemplified in the press and the speed and coordination that are highly exemplified in the snatch. The rules state that the bar must come to the chest in one movement, and after recovery from the clean, the legs are bent and then extended as the arms extend and the bar is jerked overhead. As in the snatch, there is both a split and a squat style.

Teaching the Split Style

The split style has the same forms as the split snatch, namely the equal split, the wedge split, and the hop back split. And as with the split snatch, we will teach the equal split.

The Address Position

This is the same as in the clean for the press.

The Get-Ready Position

This is the same as in the clean for the press.

First Pull

This is the same as in the clean for the press.

Second Pull

This is the same pulling motion as in the clean for the press except the elevation of the shoulders is higher and flexion of the arms is less since the second pull ends 2 - 3 inches above the waist (see picture #60).

Elbow Whip, Split and Catch

As the bar reaches 2 - 3 inches above the waist, the elbows whip and the legs split at the same time. The lifter should split as low as possible without touching his knee to the platform and with the front leg at least parallel to the ground (see picture #61). The elbow whip must be fast. It is similar to the elbow whip of the clean for the press but instead of the elbows forward at the end of the whip, the elbows are high. The catch (when the bar lands on the shoulders) must be made at the exact time the lifter reaches the bottom of his split, not one after the other.

Recovery

This is like the split snatch recovery except that the bar is at the chest instead of overhead.

Sequence of Exercises to Teach the Split Clean

Split Clean Squat Exercise

This is just like the split clean squat exercise we have been using in our preliminary work. It is very important to see that the student keeps his trunk upright or even leaning back. If he does not, it can help if you tell him to move his hips farther forward. The head should be down and the back leg should be as straight as possible. Finally, the student should be as low as possible. The front leg should be at least parallel to the ground. Do sets of 4 - 7 repetitions using light weights with 1 - 2 minutes rest between sets.

First Pull Exercise

The sequence of exercises is the same as in the clean for the the press.

Second Pull Exercise

The sequence of exercises and rest periods is the same as in the clean for the press. Remember that the second pull for the clean ends 2 - 3 inches above the waist and that the difference between the second pull for the press and the second pull for the clean part of the clean and jerk is that the shoulders are used more in the clean and the flexion of the arms is less.

High Pull Exercise

The sequence of exercises and rest periods is the same as in the clean for the press. Remember that the high pull ends 2 - 3 inches above the waist.

Elbow Whip and Small Split Exercise

Follow the same sequence as before of no weight, empty bar, and then light weights, with the same rest periods. Start with the bar a little higher than where the elbow whip would normally be started. This would be 4 - 5 inches above the waist. Now standing on the toes, extend the wrists, throw the elbows forward fast and high, and split at the same time. The depth of the split is only about 6 inches (see picture #62). Check that the bar lands on the shoulders at the same time the lifter reaches the termination of his split. This whole movement must be fast. Check that the trunk is straight and the bar was pulled straight.

Power Split Clean Exercise

This is the same as a split clean except that the student pulls the bar from the floor to 4 - 5 inches above the waist instead of to 2 - 3 inches. This means the bar is caught higher and the split is not deep, only 6 inches. Using the weight that he was using for upright rows, the student does 6 repetitions in sets with 2 minutes rest between. All repetitions are done from the platform. Watch that the student is doing things correctly as he passes through the various parts of the lift.

Split Clean Exercise

Following the sequence of no weight, bar, and light weight and using the appropriate rest intervals, do the split clean in entirety. When using light weights do sets of 3 repetitions, dead hanging the second and third repetitions. When the student can do this well, he is ready for a split clean routine.

Split Clean Routine

There are many routines from which to choose, and we must choose with the same factors present that are present in the other lifts. The following is a beginning routine.

Beginning Routine – 1 to 2 weeks

Have the student do 4 sets of 3 repetitions in the split clean and 2 sets of 3 in the high pulls with 2 minutes rest between sets. The student should start with a light weight (the weight he was using for upright rows) for the first two sets and then add weight on the following two sets. If the student misses twice in a row with a weight or shows bad form, have him use less weight. Stress form, speed and timing. All repetitions in the split clean and high pulls should be done in singles. A lot of weight can be used in the high pulls as long as the student shows he can accelerate the bar during the second pull. As the student becomes more proficient in the split style, he may adopt any of the three routines outlined for the split snatch and work according to the same principles.

Teaching the Squat Clean

Everything is the same as in the split style through the second pull. As the bar gets to its highest point the elbows are thrown forward, but at this point in the squat style the lifter squats under the bar to catch it instead of splitting under it to catch it.

Squat, Whip, and Catch

The squat is exactly like the squat in the squat snatch. The height of the elbow whip is more important in the squat than in the split clean style (see picture #63). The split lifter can rock under the weight if the elbows are not up, but a squatter can not. The split lifter can rock back to save a lift that is sliding down the chest because the elbows are forward and not back, but a squatter can not. As in the split clean catch, the catch must be made when the lifter arrives at his bottom position, not before or after.

Recovery

The recovery is the same as in the squat snatch. The same principles of height of hip and head hold true for securing the bar.

Sequences of Exercises to Teach the Squat Clean

Light Deep Front Squat Exercise

This exercise should be done keeping in mind the developing of form and flexibility. Have the lifter keep his head level or back, hips out, back straight and inclined forward, and elbows high. The lifter should strive to go lower every repetition. Have him do 4 – 7 repetitions with light weight and gradually add weight. Rest 1 – 2 minutes between sets. Remember that this exercise is not to see how much weight can be lifted.

First Pull Exercise

Use the same exercise sequence as in the clean for the press.

Second Pull Exercise

Use the same exercise sequence as in the clean for the press with the same principles used in the second pull exercise for the split clean.

High Pull Exercise

Use the same exercise sequence as in the clean for the press with the same principles as used in the second pull exercise for the split clean.

Elbow Whip and Small Squat Exercise

This is the same as the elbow whip and small split exercise described before. Use the same exercise sequence and principles with a small squat instead of a small split. Check especially that the elbows are high. The one difference is that the trunk is straight when catching the bar in the small split, and the trunk is inclined forward when catching the bar in the small squat (see picture #64). The depth of the squat is about 6 inches.

Power Squat Clean Exercise

This is the same as the power split clean exercise, using a squat instead of a split. Check that the elbows are high and trunk inclined forward. Use the same exercise sequence as in the power split clean exercise with the same principles.

Squat Clean Exercise

Use the same sequence as in the split clean exercise. When the student can do this well he is ready for a squat clean routine and may use any one of the three routines outlined for the split snatch. Work according to the same principles.

Teaching the Split Jerk

Starting Position

Assuming the bar has already been cleaned, take the position after the recovery of the clean. The back should be straight and the head level or slightly down. Looking up does not bring the shoulders under the bar for support when the bar is overhead, and also with the head back the bar has a tendency to be thrown out in front. The elbows should be forward. It is not mandatory that they be way up, but they should never be down at the sides. The feet are 4 - 6 inches apart with the toes pointed slightly out or straight ahead (see picture #65). The breath that the student took to clean should be kept through the jerk. Letting the breath out after the clean and then taking another can be done, but this usually results in the chest sinking in and providing a poor base of support for the bar. Remember that the bar is resting high on the shoulders.

Dip

With the bar in the above position, the student bends his knees until his body drops about 6 inches (see picture #66). This should be neither a very rapid nor a very slow bend. It should be a controlled lowering of the body, keeping the bar in the same position.

Body Drive

As soon as the body is lowered 6 inches, the legs and hips extend as forcefully and rapidly as possible. From the hips and legs comes the power for jerking the bar overhead. During this phase it is very important that the position as described before is maintained. Any forward inclination of the trunk or lowering of the elbows will cause the bar to go forward. This drive should carry the bar above the top of the head if the lift is to be successful (see picture #67).

Split and Arm Drive

The split and arm drive are simultaneous and take place as the bar reaches the position above the top of the head. In the split one foot goes forward and the other goes back as in the split clean or split snatch. The student should aim for a depth of split with the front leg parallel to the floor (see picture #68). The head should be level or slightly down. It is important here as in the split clean or split snatch that the front leg goes straight forward and the back leg goes straight back. Any leg crossing or splitting wide will cause a loss of balance (see picture #69). Also, as in the split clean or split snatch, it is important that both feet point slightly inward to prevent slipping.

The arms are extended vigorously straight up or slightly back but never forward. Remember that this should take place after the body drive. Many students will want to drive with the arms before they have driven with the body. The arm drive is the finishing touch and very important, succeeding only if done after the body drive.

Recovery

The recovery is the same as in the split clean or split snatch.

Sequence of Exercises to Teach the Split Jerk

Shoulder Stretching Exercise

Do 20 - 30 shoulder dislocates before jerking as this will loosen up the shoulders so that the bar will go back.

Dip and Body Drive Exercise

Do this in the sequence of no weight, bar, then light weight in sets of 4 - 7 repetitions. Light weight is a weight with which the student was doing presses for 4 - 6 repetitions. Remember the drive of the bar should only be to the top of the head. Watch closely to see that the body does not incline forward and elbows do not drop. Be sure that the student starts his dip with correct foot spacing and that the shoulders are supporting the weight (see picture #70) and not the arms (see picture #71). When using just the bar or no weight, rest 30 seconds between sets, and rest 1 - 2 minutes when using weights.

Split, Arm Drive, and Recovery Exercise

In the same sequence of no weight, bar, and light weight (the same as used for doing presses of 4 - 6 repetitions) assume a position with the bar at the top of the head (see picture #72). From this position the student will go through the split and arm drive simultaneously and then the recovery in sets of 4 - 7 repetitions with the same rest intervals as above. The bar is lowered only to the top of the head after one repetition and from there begins the next repetition. Watch closely to see that the bar is driven back, the student reaches the correct depth, and the legs split directly back and forward with the correct foot position. If everything is done correctly but the student has a bunched-up appearance, this is because his front foot did not go far enough forward nor his back foot far enough backward during the split. In this bunched-up appearance the back leg will be bent far too much (see picture #73). A slight bend is permissable. Also be sure the student's split is done close to the floor. Sometimes the student will be found jumping when he splits instead of traversing the distance to the floor.

Split Jerk Routine

Jerk from the Rack

Take a bar off the squat stands and do the jerk as described before with a light weight, the weight the student was using for presses of 4 - 6 repetitions. Do 4 sets of 3 repetitions resting 2 minutes between sets. Air is let out when the bar is extended overhead, and another breath is taken as the bar is lowered for the next repetition. Increase the weight each set by 10 - 15 pounds.

Teaching the Squat Jerk

Most lifters can not use the squat jerk because a lifter must be extraordinarily flexible in the shoulders and hips in order to use it. The author feels it has more potential than the split jerk since it is a less complex movement, quicker, and a lower position can be reached if a person is flexible enough.

Everything up to and including the drive is the same as in the split jerk. After the drive instead of splitting under the bar, the lifter bends his knees, dropping directly under the bar or dropping and shuffling forward under the bar. At the same time the arms drive straight up or slightly back. The recovery is made merely by standing up. It should be pointed out that as in the squat snatch, the hips and head play the same important role in balance. If the weight is forward, the head goes up and the hips forward. If the weight is back, the head goes down and the hips back.

Sequence of Exercises to Teach the Squat Jerk

Shoulder Stretching Exercise

Do 20 - 30 shoulder dislocates

Overhead Squat Exercise with a Jerk Grip

Do 4 sets of 8 repetitions resting 2 minutes between sets. The exercise should be done until the student can do 8 repetitions with body weight. In each repetition the thighs should be at least parallel to the floor (see picture #74).

Dip and Body Drive Exercise

This is done the same as in the split jerk.

Squat, Arm Drive, and Recovery Exercise

With the bar at the top of the head and using the sequence of no weight, bar, light weight (weight the student used for presses of 4 - 6 repetitions), do sets of 4 - 6 repetitions with the usual rest intervals. From the starting position the student drops or drops and shuffles forward under the bar as the arms drive straight up or slightly back. Recovery is made by standing up as described before. The bar is lowered only to the top of the head for the next repetition.

After successful completion of the above, have the student go on to a squat jerk routine which is the same as the split jerk routine, but squatting instead of splitting.

Clean and Jerk Together

We have been teaching the clean and jerk separately and will now put them together. Even when done together, one part may be stressed more than the other depending on what is less developed. There are many routines to follow and the choice of routine depends on what part needs the most emphasis, the clean or the jerk. Below are two routines each for: (1) equal emphasis, (2) emphasis on clean, and (3) emphasis on jerk.

Equal Emphasis Routines

3 Singles

The student does one clean and jerk, puts the bar down, does another, puts the bar down, and then does a third. He does 4 sets of 3 repetitions as just described, starting with a light weight that can be easily handled and adding 10 – 20 pounds each set. He rests 2 minutes between sets. Again stress form and do not permit more than two failures in a row; if this happens, he must drop down in weight.

Clean, 2 Jerks, Clean

The student does one clean, jerks the weight twice, and then dead hangs one clean. Again he does 4 sets resting 2 minutes between sets. He starts with a light weight and adds 10 – 20 pounds each set. Again stress form.

Clean Emphasis Routines

One and Two

The student does one clean and jerk followed by two dead hang cleans. Four sets are done with 2 minutes rest between sets. He starts with a light weight and adds 10 – 20 pounds each set. Stress form.

One and Four

The student does one clean and jerk followed by four dead hang cleans. A light weight is chosen and used during the entire routine; there is no progression in weight. This routine works very well if a student can not get the idea of the second pull. Especially emphasize going fast when the bar reaches the knees. Again he does 4 sets with 2 minute rest intervals between sets.

Jerk Emphasis Routines

One and Three

The student cleans the bar once and does three jerks. Be sure he is in good position before each jerk. Usually the student will not be in good position and, as a result, the jerks are done sloppily. Do 4 sets adding 10 - 20 pounds each set and resting 2 minutes between sets.

One and Five

The student cleans the bar once and does five jerks. There is no progression in weight. He chooses a light weight and does 4 sets with it, resting 2 minutes between sets. This routine works very well with students who have not learned to go low on their jerks. After 4 sets of 5 jerks they go low!

CHAPTER V

Example Semester Routines

Throughout the past three chapters it has been discussed how to teach the different lifts by breaking the lifts down into their different components and then building them up. Teaching sequences and routines have been suggested. The rest of the book will be devoted to putting these teaching sequences and routines into three different class schedules, a continuation of the schedules found in Chapter One. The first schedule is for classes 3 days a week, 30 - 40 minutes each class. The second schedule is for classes 2 days a week, 45 -60 minutes each class. The third schedule is for classes 4 days a week, 30 - 40 minutes each class. If the teacher does not have a class schedule that is the same as one of these, he can use his imagination to arrange one of them to fit his own individual schedule.

3 Days a Week, 30 - 40 Minutes

Preliminary Work – 5 weeks

This is described in Chapter One.

Teaching the Olympic Lifts – the rest of the semester (10 weeks)

1 st Week

1 st Workout

Stretching Exercises – 5 minutes

Sequence of Exercises to Teach the Clean for the Press – 20 to 25 minutes

When the student has learned the clean, have him practice it in sets of 6 repetitions in singles with light weights.

Front Squats – 10 to 12 minutes

Do 4 sets of 6 repetitions. In these and all front squats in following workouts the student starts with light weight and adds weight each set.

2 nd Workout

Stretching Exercises – 5 minutes

Review – 10 minutes

Do the sequence of exercises to teach the clean for the press.

Sequence of Exercises to Teach the Press – 15 to 20 minutes

When the student has learned the press, have him practice it in sets of 6 repetitions with light weight. If time permits, do sets of 6 repetitions of the front squat.

3 rd Workout

Stretching Exercises – 5 minutes

Clean and Press – 10 to 12 minutes

Do 4 sets of 6 repetitions of both the clean and the press. Start light and add 5 pounds each set.

Front Squats – 10 to 15 minutes

Do 4 or 5 sets of 6 repetitions.

2 nd Week

4 th Workout

Sequence of Exercises to Teach the Split Snatch – 25 minutes

Clean and Press – 10 to 12 minutes

Do the same as in the third workout.

5 th Workout

Review – 25 minutes

Do the sequence of exercises to teach the split snatch.

Front Squats

With the remaining time do as many sets of front squats as possible.

6 th Workout

Sequence of Exercises to Teach the Split Snatch – 25 minutes

Clean and Press – 5 minutes

Do the same as in the third workout, but do only 2 sets instead of 4.

Front Squats – 5 minutes

Do 2 sets of 6 repetitions.

3 rd Week

7 th Workout

Review – 20 minutes

Do the sequence of exercises to teach the split clean.

Sequence of Exercises to Teach the Split Jerk – 15 minutes

8 th Workout

Stretching Exercises 5 minutes

Beginning Split Snatch Routine – 20 minutes

Clean and Press – 5 minutes

Do the same as in the third workout, but do only 2 sets instead of 4.

Front Squats – 5 minutes

Do 2 sets of 6 repetitions

9th Workout

Stretching Exercises – 5 minutes

Beginning Split Clean Routine – 20 minutes

Jerk off the Rack – 10 minutes

Do 4 sets of 3 repetitions with light weight.

4 th Week

10th Workout

Stretching Exercises – 5 minutes

Beginning Split Snatch Routine – 15 minutes

Beginning Press Routine – 10 to 12 minutes

Front Squats – 8 to 10 minutes

Do 3 sets of 6 repetitions.

11th Workout

This is the same as the tenth workout except that the student does the Beginning Split Clean Routine (15 minutes) instead of the Beginning Split Snatch Routine.

12th Workout

This is the same as the tenth workout.

5 th Week

13th Workout

Stretching Exercises – 5 minutes

Clean Emphasis Routine – 15 minutes

Choose one of the two clean and jerk routines in which emphasis is on the clean. Use the split style. Use this routine from now on when Clean Emphasis Routine is stated. Following this routine do 2 sets of 3 repetitions in the high pull.

Beginning Press Routine – 10 to 12 minutes

Front Squats – 8 to 10 minutes

Do 3 sets of 6 repetitions.

14th Workout

This is the same as the thirteenth workout except that the student does a Split Snatch Routine (15 minutes) instead of a Clean Emphasis Routine. Choose one of the split snatch routines. Use this routine from now on whenever Split Snatch Routine is stated.

15th Workout

This is the same as the thirteenth workout. This workout is a good time to test the maximum for 6 repetitions in the press.

6 th Week

16th Workout

Sequence of Exercises to Teach the Squat Snatch - 25 minutes

Front Squats - 10 to 12 minutes

Do 4 sets of 6 repetitions.

17th Workout

Review - 20 minutes

Do the sequence of exercises to teach the squat snatch.

Press Routine - 15 minutes

Choose one of the press routines that can be done after the beginning routine. Use this routine from now on whenever Press Routine is stated.

18th Workout

Sequence of Exercises to Teach the Squat Clean - 25 minutes

Front Squats - 10 to 12 minutes

Do 4 sets of 6 repetitions.

7 th Week

19th Workout

Review – 20 minutes

Do the sequence of exercises to teach the squat clean.

Press Routine – 15 minutes

20th Workout

Overhead Squats – 10 minutes

Do 3 sets of 8 repetitions with light weights.

Complete Squat Snatch – 10 minutes

Do 4 sets of 6 repetitions with light weights. Each repetition is from the floor.

Press Routine – 15 minutes

21st Workout

Stretching Exercises – 5 minutes

Beginning Squat Clean Routine – 15 minutes

Jerk off the Rack – 10 minutes

Do 4 sets of 3 repetitions.

Front Squats – 8 to 10 minutes

Do 3 sets of 6 repetitions.

8 th Week

22nd Workout

Stretching Exercises – 5 minutes

Beginning Squat Snatch Routine – 15 minutes

Press Routine – 15 minutes

Front Squats – 5 minutes

Do 2 sets of 6 repetitions.

23rd Workout

This is the same as the twenty-second workout except that the student does the Beginning Squat Clean Routine (15 minutes) instead of the Beginning Squat Snatch

Routine.

24th Workout

This is the same as the twenty-second workout.

9th Week

25th Workout

Stretching Exercises – 5 minutes

Clean Emphasis Routine – 15 minutes

Use the squat style. Following this do 2 sets of 3 repetitions in the high pull.

Press Routine – 15 minutes

Front Squats – 5 minutes

Do 2 sets of 6 repetitions.

26th Workout

This is the same as the twenty-fifth workout except that the student does a Squat Snatch Routine (15 minutes) instead of a Clean Emphasis Routine. Choose one of the squat snatch routines and use it from now on where Squat Snatch Routine is stated. However, the student does not begin this routine until he can overhead squat 8 repetitions with 60 - 65% of his body weight. If he still can not do this after 1½ weeks, he will start the squat snatch routine anyway. Each time this routine is done, it should be preceded by 1 set of 8 repetitions with 50% body weight.

27th Workout

This is the same as the twenty-fifth workout.

10th Week

This tenth and last week the teacher may devote to testing. Those students not being tested while another student (or students) is being tested will continue with the workout for that session. It is suggested that the following be tested; (1) Squat Clean and Jerk, (2) Squat Snatch, (3) Split Clean and Jerk, (4) Split Snatch, and (5) Press. There should be one test to test maximum for one repetition for each of the above and one test to test the form of the above. The student should receive two grades for each lift, one for form and the other for the amount of weight lifted. It is suggested that the Front **Squat** also be judged but only for the amount of weight lifted for 6 repetitions (and not **for** form).

Because of the differences in body weight, each lifter should be equated according to body weight. The fairest method known to the author is the Bob Hoffman Formula which can be found at the back of this book.

28th Workout

This is the same as the twenty-sixth workout.

29th Workout

This is the same as the twenty-fifth workout.

30th Workout

This is the same as the twenty-sixth workout.

2 Days a Week, 45 – 60 Minutes

Preliminary Work – 5 weeks

This is described in Chapter One.

Teaching the Olympic Lifts – the rest of the semester (10 weeks)

1 st Week

1 st Workout

Stretching Exercises – 5 minutes

Sequence of Exercises to Teach the Clean for the Press – 30 minutes

When the student has learned the clean, have him practice it in sets of 6 repetitions in singles with light weights.

Front Squats – 15 to 20 minutes

Do 5 or 6 sets of 6 repetitions. In these and all front squats in following workouts the student starts with light weight and adds weight each set.

2 nd Workout

Stretching Exercises - 5 minutes

Review - 10 minutes

Do the sequence of exercises to teach the clean for the press.

Sequence of Exercises to Teach the Press - 20 minutes

When the student has learned the press, have him practice it in sets of 6 repetitions with weight.

Clean and Press - 10 to 12 minutes

Do 4 sets of 6 repetitions of both the clean and the press. Start light and add 5 pounds each set.

Front Squats - 10 to 12 minutes

Do 4 sets of 6 repetitions.

2 nd Week

3 rd Workout

Sequence of Exercises to Teach the Split Snatch - 30 minutes

Clean and Press - 10 to 12 minutes

Do the same as in the second workout.

Front Squats - 10 to 12 minutes

Do 4 sets of 6 repetitions.

4 th Workout

Review - 20 minutes

Do the sequence of exercises to teach the split snatch.

Sequence of Exercises to Teach the Split Clean - 30 minutes

Clean and Press - 5 minutes

Do 2 sets of 6 repetitions.

Front Squats - 5 minutes

Do 2 sets of 6 repetitions.

3 rd Week

5 th Workout

Review - 20 minutes

Do the sequence of exercises to teach the split clean.

Sequence of Exercises to Teach the Split Jerk - 15 minutes

Beginning Split Clean Routine - 20 minutes

6 th Workout

Stretching Exercises - 5 minutes

Beginning Split Snatch Routine - 20 minutes

Clean and Press - 7 to 9 minutes

Do 3 sets of 6 repetitions.

Jerk off the Rack - 10 minutes

Do 4 sets of 3 repetitions with light weight.

Front Squats - 8 to 10 minutes

Do 3 sets of 6 repetitions.

4 th Week

7 th Workout

Stretching Exercises - 5 minutes

Beginning Split Snatch Routine - 20 to 22 minutes

Do 2 sets of high pulls in addition to the high pulls in the routine.

Beginning Press Routine - 10 to 12 minutes

Front Squats - 10 to 12 minutes

Do 4 sets of 6 repetitions.

8 th Workout

This is the same as the seventh workout except that the student does the Beginning Split Clean Routine (20 to 22 minutes) instead of the Beginning Split Snatch Routine. Do 2 sets of high pulls in addition to the high pulls in the routine.

5 th Week

9 th Workout

Stretching Exercises – 5 minutes

Split Snatch Routine – 20 to 22 minutes

Choose one of the split snatch routines. Do 2 additional sets of high pulls.

Beginning Press Routine – 10 to 12 minutes

Front Squats – 10 to 12 minutes

Do 4 sets of 6 repetitions.

10th Workout

This is the same as the ninth workout except that the student does a clean Emphasis Routine (20 to 22 minutes) instead of a split snatch routine. Choose one of the two clean and jerk routines in which emphasis is on the clean. Use the split style. Use this routine from now on when Clean Emphasis Routine is stated. In addition, do 4 sets of 3 repetitions of high pull.

This workout is a good time to test the maximum for 6 repetitions in the press.

6 th Week

11th Workout

Sequence of Exercises to Teach the Squat Snatch – 30 minutes

The squat snatch requires much learning of balance. If the instructor finishes the sequence before 30 minutes are up, he should have his students practice the complete squat snatch with an empty bar. This should be done in singles.

Press Routine – 15 minutes

Choose one of the press routines that can be done after the beginning routine. Do this routine from now on whenever Press Routine is stated.

Front Squats – 10 to 12 minutes

Do 4 sets of 6 repetitions.

7 th Week

13th Workout

Review – 20 minutes

Do the sequence of exercises to teach the squat clean.

Overhead Squats – 10 minutes

Do 3 sets of 8 repetitions with light weights.

Complete Squat Snatch – 10 minutes

Do 4 sets of 6 repetitions with light weights. Each repetition is from the floor.

Press Routine – 15 minutes

14th Workout

Stretching Exercises – 5 minutes

Beginning Squats Routine – 15 minutes

Jerk off the Rack – 10 minutes

Press Routine – 15 minutes

Front Squats – 8 to 10 minutes

Do 3 sets of 6 repetitions.

8 th Week

15th Workout

Stretching Exercises – 5 minutes

Beginning Squat Snatch Routine – 20 to 22 minutes

Do 2 sets of high pulls in addition to the high pulls in the routine.

Press Routine – 15 minutes

Front Squats – 10 to 12 minutes

Do 4 sets of 6 repetitions.

16th Workout

This is the same as the fifteenth workout except that the student does the Beginning Squat Clean Routine (20 to 22 minutes) instead of the Beginning Squat Snatch Routine. Do 2 sets of high pulls in addition to the high pulls in the routine.

9th Week

17th Workout

Stretching Exercises – 5 minutes

Squat Snatch Routine – 20 to 22 minutes

Choose one of the squat snatch routines. Do 2 additional sets of high pulls. The student does not begin this routine until he can overhead squat 8 repetitions with 60 - 65% of his body weight. If he still can not do this after 1½ weeks, he will start the squat snatch routine anyway. Each time this routine is done, it should be preceded by 1 set of 8 repetitions with 50% body weight.

Press Routine – 15 minutes

Front Squats – 10 to 12 minutes

Do 4 sets of 6 repetitions.

18th Workout

This is the same as the seventeenth workout except that the student does the Clean Emphasis Routine (20 to 22 minutes) instead of the Squat Snatch Routine. Use the squat style. Follow with 4 sets of 3 repetitions of high pulls.

10th Week

This tenth and last week the teacher may devote to testing. Those students not being tested while another student (or students) is being tested will continue with the workout for that session. This testing is the same as described in the tenth week of the 3 day a week schedule.

19th Workout

This is the same as the seventeenth workout.

20th Workout

This is the same as the eighteenth workout.

4 Days a Week, 30 - 40 Minutes

Preliminary Work - 4 weeks

This is described in Chapter One.

Teaching the Olympic Lifts -the rest of the semester (10 to 11 weeks)

1 st Week

1 st Workout

Stretching Exercises - 5 minutes

Sequence of Exercises to Teach the Clean for the Press - 20 to 25 minutes

When the student has learned the clean, have him practice it in sets of 6 repetitions in singles with light weights.

Front Squats - 10 to 12 minutes

Do 4 sets of 6 repetitions. In these and all front squats in following workouts the student starts with light weight and adds weight each set.

2 nd Workout

Stretching Exercises - 5 minutes

Sequence of Exercises to Teach the Press - 15 to 20 minutes

When the student has learned the press, have him practice it in sets of 6 repetitions with light weight.

3 rd Workout

Stretching Exercises - 5 minutes

Clean and Press - 10 to 12 minutes

Do 4 sets of 6 repetitions of both the clean and the press. Start light and add 5 pounds each set.

Front Squats – 15 to 20 minutes

Do 5 or 6 sets of 6 repetitions.

4 th Workout

Sequence of Exercises to Teach the Split Snatch – 25 minutes

Front Squats – 10 to 12 minutes

Do 4 sets of 6 repetitions. Use a lighter weight than used in the third workout and concentrate on good form.

2 nd Week

5 th Workout

Review – 20 minutes

Do the sequence of exercises to teach the split snatch.

Clean and Press – 10 to 12 minutes

Do the same as in the third workout.

6 th Workout

Sequence of Exercises to Teach the Split Clean – 25 minutes

Front Squats – 10 to 12 minutes

Do 4 sets of 6 repetitions.

7 th Workout

Review – 20 minutes

Do the sequence of exercises to teach the split clean.

Sequence of Exercises to Teach the Split Jerk – 15 minutes

8 th Workout

Stretching Exercises – 5 minutes

Beginning Split Snatch Routine – 20 minutes

Front Squats – 10 to 12 minutes

    Do 4 sets of 6 repetitions.

3 rd Week

9 th Workout

Stretching Exercises – 5 minutes

Beginning Split Clean Routine – 20 minutes

Jerk off the Rack – 10 minutes

    Do 4 sets of 3 repetitions with light weights.

10th Workout

Stretching Exercises – 5 minutes

Beginning Split Snatch Routine – 15 minutes

Beginning Press Routine – 10 to 12 minutes

Front Squats – 8 to 10 minutes

    Do 3 sets of 6 repetitions.

11th Workout

    This is the same as the tenth workout except that the student does the Beginning Split Clean Routine (15 minutes) instead of the Beginning Split Snatch Routine.

12th Workout

    This is the same as the tenth workout.

4 th Week

13th Workout

    This is the same as the eleventh workout.

14th Workout

Stretching Exercises – 5 minutes

Split Snatch Routine – 15 minutes

Choose one of the split snatch routines.

Beginning Press Routine – 10 to 12 minutes

Front Squats – 8 to 10 minutes

Do 3 sets of 6 repetitions.

15th Workout

This is the same as the fourteenth workout except that the student does a Clean Emphasis Routine (15 minutes) instead of the Split Snatch Routine. Choose one of the two clean and jerk routines in which emphasis is on the clean. Use the split style. Use this routine from now on whenever Clean Emphasis Routine is stated. Follow this routine with 2 sets of 3 repetitions of high pulls.

16th Workout

This in the same as the fourteenth workout.

5 th Week

17th and 19th Workouts

These are the same as the fifteenth workout.

18th and 20th Workouts

These are the same as the fourteenth workout.

6 th Week

21st and 23rd Workouts

These are the same as the fifteenth workout.

22nd and 24th Workouts

These are the same as the fourteenth workout.

7th Week

25th Workout

Sequence of Exercises to Teach the Squat Snatch – 25 minutes

Front Squats – 10 to 12 minutes

Do 4 sets of 6 repetitions.

26th Workout

Review – 20 minutes

Do the sequence of exercises to teach the squat snatch.

Press Routine – 15 minutes

Choose one of the press routines that can be done after the beginning routine. Do this routine from now on whenever Press Routine is stated.

27th Workout

Sequence of Exercises to Teach the Squat Clean – 25 minutes

Front Squats – 10 to 12 minutes

Do 4 sets of 6 repetitions.

28th Workout

Review – 20 minutes

Press Routine – 15 minutes

8 th Week

Workouts should start with stretching exercises if stretching is not included in the first exercise done.

29th Workout

Overhead Squats – 10 minutes

Do 3 sets of 8 repetitions with light weights.

Complete Squat Snatch – 10 minutes

Do 4 sets of 6 repetitions with light weights. Each repetition is from the floor.

Press Routine – 15 minutes

Deep Bouncing Squat (♯1) Student stays in this position and bounces up and down.

Split Squat(♯2) Each leg is forward for one set.

Bench Press (♯3) Student pauses at chest for one second.

Incline Press (♯4)

Upright Row (♯5) The bar is pulled to this height.

Front Squat (♯6) The bar is Supported entirely by the shoulders. This can be done if the elbows are high as shown in the picture.

Front Squat(# 7) The legs are bent until the thighs are parallel to the floor.

Trunk to Thigh Touch with Foot on Bench (# 8)

Shoulder Dislocate (# 9) This is the initial position. From here the towel or broom handle is lowered back with the arms remaining straight.

Shoulder Dislocate (#10) This is the end position. From here the towel or broom handle is raised to the initial position with the arms remaining straight. As the shoulders get looser the hands may be placed closer together.

Feet Crossed Toe Touch (#11) The first set is done with the right foot over the left and the next set with the left foot over the right.

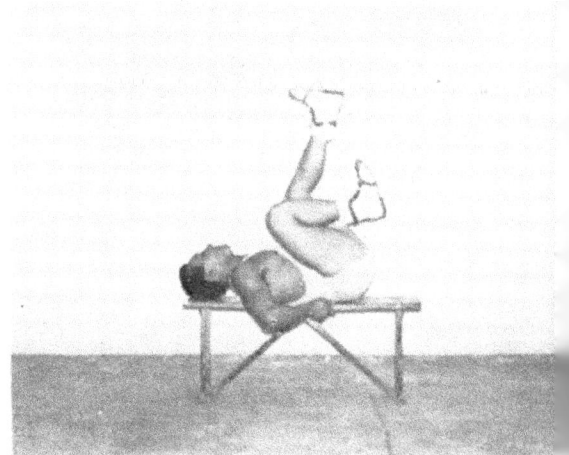

Bicycle Pump (#12)

Squat Jump (#13) From this position the student jumps straight up.

Squat Jump (#14) After being in the air, as pictured, the student returns to the initial position.

Split Clean Squat (#15) This is just like the Split Squat but here a bar is supported on the shoulders.

Split Snatch Squat (#16) This is just like the Split Squat but here a bar is held over the head with a wide grip.

Overhead Squat with Bar (#17)

Jumping Alternate Split (#18) From this position the student leaps into the air and splits, landing in the split position. He returns to the initial position for the next leap.

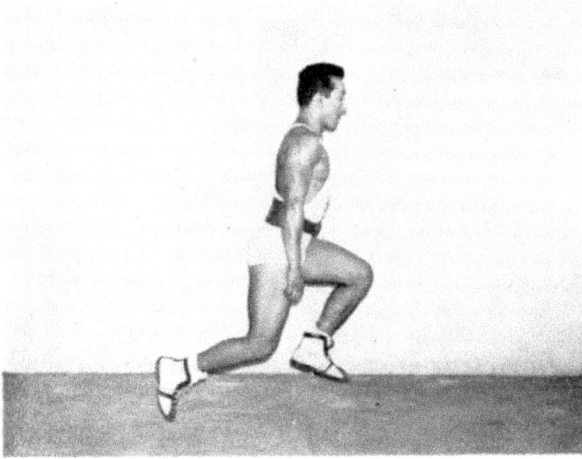

Jumping Alternate Split (#19) Each time the student leaps he reverses feet, putting in front the foot that was in back the previous leap, and putting in back the one that was in front.

Throw Arms to Chest as Split, Alternating Front Legs (#20) From this position the student extends legs rapidly to standing position and splits rapidly throwing arms to chest.

Throw Arms to Chest as Split, Alternating Front Legs (#21) This is the end position. From here the student goes back to the initial position for the next split in which the opposite leg goes forward.

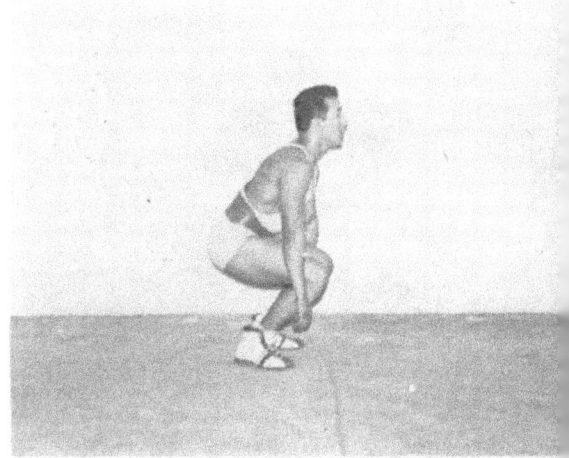

Throw Arms Overhead as Squat (#22) From this position the student extends legs rapidly to standing position and throws arms overhead as he squats rapidly.

Throw Arms Overhead as Squat (#23) This is the end position.

Bouncing Front Squat with Light Weight (#24) This is just like the Deep Bouncing Squat but here a weight is supported on the shoulders.

Throw Arms to Chest as Squat (#25) From this position the student extends legs rapidly to standing position and throws arms to chest as he squats rapidly.

Throw Arms to Chest as Squat (#26) This is the end position.

Throw Arms Overhead as Split, Alternating Front Legs (#27) From this position the student extends legs rapidly to standing position and throws arms overhead as he splits rapidly.

Throw Arms Overhead as Split, Alternating Front Legs (#28) This is the end position. From here the student goes back to the initial position for the next split with the opposite leg going forward.

Two Arms Curl (#29)

Passable Press (#30)

Lean Back Style Press (#31) The lifter starts in lean back position with a wide grip and remains there as he presses the weight.

Initial Position of Garcy Style or Russian Style Press (#32) This is very similar to the Lean Back Style except that in this style the grip is narrower and the lifter does not remain leaning back throughout the press.

Position After the Bar is Thrown Off the Chest (#33) Notice that the chest has come forward and the hips, thighs, and stomach have gone back.

Position After the Bar Has Been Caught Above the Hairline (#34) From here the bar is pressed and the body comes slowly erect.

Address Position for the Clean for the Press (#35)

Hook Grip (#36)

et Ready Position in the Clean for the Press (#37)

First Pull in the Clean for the Press (#38)
From the floor the bar is pulled to knee height
which marks the end of the first pull.

econd Pull in the Clean for the Press (#39) The
cond pull is from knee height to this height.

Elbow Whip and Dip in the Clean for the Press (#40)
Here the student is throwing his elbows underneath
the bar and is bending his legs.

Elbow Whip and Dip in the Clean for the Press (#41)
Here is the finish of the elbow whip and dip. The
student now straightens his legs and is ready to press
the weight.

Second Pull Exercise in the Clean for the Press (#42)
The arms should be straight at the start of the second
pull so that the big muscles of the back. legs, and
hips can start the pulling.

Second Pull Exercise in the Clean for the Press (#43)
The arms should not be bent like this at the beginning
of this exercise.

High Pull Exercise in the Clean for the Press (#44)
From the floor the bar is pulled to this height
passing through the stages of first and second pull.
Emphasis is on accelerating the bar at the start of
the second pull (knee height).

Elbow Whip and Dip Exercise in the Clean for the
Press (#45) The student assumes this position and
goes through the exercise.

Initial Drive in the Press (#46) The arms drive
and the hips and legs move forward as the chest
and head move back.

Initial Drive in the Press (#47) Do not let the student
throw the bar away from the face during the initial
drive as is shown here.

Follow Through Exercise in the Press (#48) The
student must not fall away from the bar as is
shown here.

Get Ready Position in the Snatch (#49) Notice the wide grip. The width depends on the tightness of the student's shoulders; the tighter the shoulders, the wider the grip.

First Pull in the Snatch (#50)

Second Pull in the Snatch(#51)

Split and Flip in the Split Snatch (#52) The splitting of the legs is being done simultaneously with the extension of the wrists and arms.

Split and Flip in the Split Snatch (#53) The bar is secured and the student is in a low position. Notice the trunk is straight with the hips under the trunk and the bar over the head or a little back. The bar should never be in a forward position over the head.

Recovery in the Split Snatch (#54) The front foot is brought back first, then the back foot brought forward, and then the process repeated as the student recovers from the low position.

Recovery in the Split Snatch(#55)

Dead Hang （#56） In a dead hang the bar is alwa returned to an area around the knees and then pull up again for the next repetition.

Squat and Flip in the Squat Snatch (#57) The student is up on his toes ready to squat and flip the bar.

Squat and Flip in the Squat Snatch （#58） The ba has been secured and the student is in a deep squ position. The bar is back in this picture so the hi are out and the head is down. If the bar we forward this would be reversed.

Flip and Small Squat Exercise in the Squat Snatch (#59) The student has dropped only about 6 inches.

Second Pull in the Clean and Jerk (#60) The bar is part way through the second pull and continues to 2 or 3 inches above the waist.

Elbow Whip, Split and Catch in the Split Clean (#61)
The bar is caught and the student is in a low
position.

Elbow Whip, Split and Catch Exercise in the Split
Clean (#62)   The student has dropped only about
6 inches.

Squat Whip and Catch in the Squat Clean (#63)
The lifter has caught the bar and is in a good position
to rise.   Notice the high elbows.

Elbow Whip and Small Squat Exercise in the Squat
Clean (#64)

Starting Position of the Split Jerk (#65)

Dip in the Split Jerk (#66)   The dip is about 6
inches.

Body Drive in the Split Jerk (#67) The drive carries the bar above the top of the head.

Split and Arm Drive in the Split Jerk (#68) The front leg is parallel to the floor.

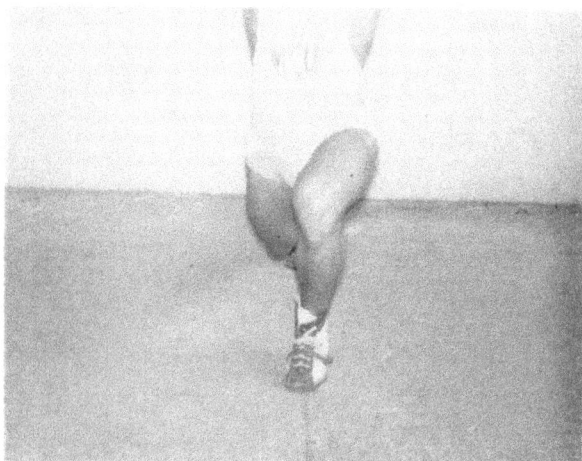

Split and Arm Drive in the Split Jerk (#69) The lifter's legs have not gone straight back and forward but have gone inward and a loss of balance will result. Loss of balance will also result if the legs go outward. They must split straight forward and back.

Dip and Drive Exercise in the Split Jerk (#70) This is a good position; the shoulders are support ing the weight and foot spacing is correct.

Dip and Drive Exercise in the Split Jerk (#71) This is a bad position because the arms are supporting the weight.

Split Arm Drive, and Recovery Exercise in the Split Jerk (#72) Each repetition starts and ends with this position.

Split, Arm Drive, and Recovery Exercise in the Split Jerk (#73) The student has this bunched-up appearance when he has not split wide enough.

Overhead Squat Exercise with a Jerk Grip in the Squat Jerk (#74) The student squats with the top of the thighs parallel to the floor.

THE BOB HOFFMAN FORMULA

The Hoffman Formula has been used all over the world for a quarter of a century and has been proven to be the best way to compare one lifter's ability with that of another and to compare one record with another. It is used as a basis of determining the "Best Lifter Award" in championship lifting. It has been adopted by the A.A.U. and appears in the A.A.U. rule book.

If the weight of a lifter contains a fraction and this fraction is less than ½, it shall count as the lowest pound, and if more than ½, the next highest poundage will be counted. For example, 181¼ would be 181, and 181¾ would be 182. To make a comparison between two lifers, use the cofficient which corresponds to the lifter's bodyweight, and multiply this by the lifting total of the lifter. To compare one record with another, multiply the lifter's coefficient by the record he has established, To compare a lighter lifter with a heavier one, divide the lighter coefficient by the heavier, and then multiply the resulting figure by the lighter man's total and see how it compares with the heavier man's total. To obtain the coefficient for a man heavier than 210, deduct .001 from .669 for each pound of bodyweight over 210.

110	1.000								
111	.994	121	.935	131	.885	141	.840	151	.800
112	.988	122	.930	132	.881	142	˙836	152	.797
113	.982	123	.925	133	.876	143	.832	153	.793
114	.976	124	.920	134	.872	144	.828	154	.790
115	.970	125	.915	135	.867	145	.824	155	.786
116	.964	126	.910	136	.863	146	.820	156	.783
117	.958	127	.905	137	.858	147	.816	157	.779
118	.952	128	.900	138	.854	148	.812	158	.776
119	.946	129	.895	139	.849	149	.808	159	.772
120	.940	130	.890	140	.844	150	.804	160	.769

161	.766	171	.736	181	.712	191	.692	201	.678
162	.763	172	.734	182	.710	192	.691	202	.677
163	.760	173	.731	183	.708	193	.689	203	.676
164	.757	174	.729	184	.706	194	.688	204	.675
165	.754	175	.726	185	.704	195	.686	205	.674
166	.751	176	.724	186	.702	196	.685	206	.673
167	.748	177	.721	187	.700	197	.683	207	.672
168	.745	178	.719	188	.698	198	.682	208	.671
169	.742	179	.716	189	.696	199	.680	209	.670
170	.739	180	.714	190	.694	200	.679	210	.669